Table Of Con~~tents~~

Introduction

First of all, I want to say "Thank you" for downloading/purchasing the book and for taking the time to improve your quality of life.

The "Evernote" phenomenon is growing fast, just like Facebook, just like other viral applications, software, or websites.

This application is truly unique. It has the power to change your life, and like other heavy users say, the more you use it, the more you get out of it.

Not only can you find unlimited ways of using this app for de-cluttering and organizing your life, but while you do that, developers will also find more ways to improve it and add more features to it.

It has become my go-to app when it comes to working, productivity, and traveling. It has become my all-in-one business *application that helps me grow my entire business. All I have to say about it is that it has immense potential!*

In this guide, I will show you exactly what you need to know to use it properly – I will be concise, I will show you a few tricks, and I will illustrate the process of setting it up properly.

Who is this book for?

If you are 20 years old, you already use the app a lot and you are advanced in computers and technology, you may find this too easy and probably useless.

I created this book mainly for people who don't know anything about Evernote or for those who are just basic users – people who just write down a few notes without taking advantage of the real potential of the application.

This guide is designed to be understood by anyone and I am more than sure that you will get used to it in 90 minutes or less, just by going through this small guide.

Without further ado, let's get right into the meat!

Chapter 1: Why Evernote?

The world is constantly evolving, people are constantly evolving, and technology is constantly improving.

One of the best digital applications available for mobile phones, tablets, laptops, and desktop PCs is Evernote. Evernote is a digital notebook with the possibility of storing unlimited notes, emails, pictures, and data we use every day.

So, why should we use Evernote?

It's fast

The application itself runs very quickly, it requires a low amount of RAM and storage to run, it can be installed within a minute, it syncs everything lightning fast every time you turn on the Wi Fi, 3G, 4G, or any Internet connectivity. Notes, notebooks, and stacks are created instantaneously.

It's easy to use

Even a 7 year old kid can use it to write and play on it. It can be used for anything, especially for writing down ideas, drafts, editing documents, or writing eBooks (like I'm doing right now on my iPad). It doesn't require you to know anything special to get started, but it will require several days to learn everything about it and use it like a *pro*.

It's complex

Web clipping, email forwarding, decluttering, organizing documents, converting notes into a presentation, storing photos and important payment receipts, reminders, etc., are just few of the applications of this piece of software. More will be presented in the next chapters.

It syncs automatically on all your devices

If you are in the subway and you had a great idea, if you write it down on your phone, it will be automatically synced once you open your PC. You can work while you travel, on the go, and everything will be ready to continue once you decide to continue working on your PC.

You can set specific reminders

Every note comes standard with a reminder - you can edit it, reschedule it, or delete it if you don't need it. If you work on different projects, setting deadlines and reminders is crucial for obtaining maximum productivity.

You can share your notes with other users

Share your thoughts, notes, or notebooks with other users, friends, or colleagues with one click. If you work with several people on the same project, Evernote is the best way to communicate with them.

You can capture and store moments within Evernote

Don't let any occasion get away! Take a photo and attach it to your Evernote. Also, don't forget to write down something about it, so you won't lose any details.

You can keep everything secure

Premium and Plus plans allow you to set passcodes when accessing Evernote, so your data is secured.

It's affordable, even free for basic users

If you have any doubts about this piece of software, you can try it out for free, but keep in mind that the functions are limited. If you want all the features to be available, purchase the plus or the premium plan.

It's available for all the platforms - Android, Windows, iOS, and Mac OS

Don't worry, if you are working on just one of the platforms mentioned, Evernote is available for all of them and it syncs easily with all of them. All you need to do is to install it.

It's constantly growing and improving, reaching new users all over the world

Evernote is growing fast. To be honest, I've been using it for about 6 months, 4 months of which for free. I have purchased the Plus plan, as it fulfills my needs and I am personally in love with this app.

It's environmentally friendly

Enough with cutting trees and writing on traditional notebooks. The 21st century is the start of the paperless era. Digital information is the future and it's constantly taking the place of traditional information - books, notebooks, magazines, newspapers, etc. Our world is slowly shifting to becoming completely digital, and it's normal to be that way - it's faster, environmentally friendly, and easier for everyone.

Do you need any more reasons *not to* install and use this app? I'm an entrepreneur, a writer, and an author, and I work only online. I've using all kinds of apps for productivity, and Evernote is by far the best one. This book you are reading was written entirely using Evernote and the final notes are exported to Microsoft Word, edited, and uploaded on Kindle. I use it because it allows me to work even when I wait for my dinner to be served at restaurants or when I am waiting in queues to buy things.

It's the best choice for writers, travelers, entrepreneurs, and anyone who wants to be organized. Get your free plan by clicking here.

Chapter 2: Basic Users - Free Plan

This software application sounds really complicated based on the previous description, right? But I'll tell you what, it's really simple.

To download the application, simply click here:

https://evernote.com/download

Now, sign up by putting in the email address and username, and choose a password, and you're good to go.

Now, let's get into the meat, what you can access with the simplest plan, which is free for everyone:

1. ***You can start taking notes*** - Just simply click here to start adding notes. You can play with fonts, colors, and you can add boxes and tick them (I like that a lot).

2. ***You can create notebooks*** – A pile of notes is what will create a notebook. It can actually become a real notebook, let's take an example – Mathematics – you can put notes with different formulas, homework, equations, etc. You can arrange your notes and notebooks how you want.

3. ***You can upload up to 60MB of data/month*** – Remember, you can add 60MB of data each month, but that's not the maximum amount of

data you can store. Usually, it's almost impossible to fill that space if you just add text. Things change significantly if you add photos or other things that will increase the size of documents. The first chapter of this book has been written in Evernote and it's plain text – it was 2 KB.

4. *You can share notes or talk to other Evernote users* – All you need to do is to go to the *Work Chat* and add your friend's email (that he used to sign up to Evernote).

5. *Sync across all your devices* – You can sync your desktop PC, laptop, tablet, and smartphone. Whenever you take a note on any of them, everything will automatically sync.

6. *Set reminders for each individual note* – You can use this if you have deadlines or you just want to keep an eye on your notes or your overall progress.

7. *Create shortcuts for most frequently used notes* – If you have already created many notes but you need quick access to some of them, drag and drop them into the *shortcuts* section.

8. *The maximum size for one note is 25MB* – You can upload audio files, texts, or images, but the overall size cannot exceed this size. It will increase by upgrading to the next plans.

These are the features that are available free for everyone. If you want to have access to more features, you need to upgrade to Plus, which is $9.99/year, or Premium, which is $19.99/year.

Both plans can be paid monthly if they seem too expensive, but I guess everyone who wants this software will pay once a year.

Chapter 3: Plus Plan

If you started using Evernote on a daily basis and you need additional features, including additional storage each month, then the Evernote Plus Pricing Plan fits you.

To be honest, this is the plan that I'm currently using, and it fits me perfectly. I live in Europe, in Romania, and I need to pay 50 RON per year for that plan, which is equivalent to $12.5/year. In the United States, the plan is cheaper, around $9.99/year, and you can also pay it monthly (but I don't recommend doing that, it's 40% more expensive).

So, what benefits do you get from the Evernote Plus Plan?

The 4 most important things that you get are:

1. *Storage* – You can upload up to 1GB/month, which is 17 times more than you can upload in the Free Plan (60 MB/month).

2. *Offline Access* – This is the best feature that you get. Whenever you travel by plane or you don't have Internet access and you want to write something down, an idea, an image or an email, you can directly access your phone or your tablet or your laptop to write it. With the Free Plan, you don't have this feature, so you need to be

connected to the Internet to access Evernote.

3. *Save emails to Evernote* – You can use Web Clipper (I will cover this later on) and save your emails as texts, articles, or screenshots directly into your notes.

4. *Passcode* – You can set a custom passcode on your tablet or smartphone, just in case someone takes your phone and wants to access your Evernote app. The passcode is different than the one you normally set for your smartphone. You can use the same password, but it's not recommended.

5. *Note size* – By purchasing the Plus Plan, the maximum size of a single note increases from 25MB to 50MB.

This will allow you to store more important data or media (such as screenshots or audio files). Generally, I find 25MB to be more than enough for one note, but you never know when you need more.

Note - You can use Web Clipper through the Free Plan, too, but because of the small amount of data that you can upload on a monthly basis, you are really limited in using this feature – you will run out of data quickly.

I use all these features all the time. I am actually writing all my eBooks using Evernote. Every idea that comes into my mind when I am not at my desk, I write down and when I get home, I can continue working on it. The Premium Plan is for business people or for those who use Evernote all the time, every hour.

The whole idea here is to pick the plan that fits you best. As the Free Plan is nice to start and easy to use for everyone, I find it too basic and very limited, so my choice was Evernote Plus Plan. It's worth the money and worth using it for my own online business.

In the next chapters, I will discuss plugins, apps that connect directly with Evernote, and some tricks that can improve the user experience and productivity with this app.

Chapter 4: Premium Plan

If you're the kind of guy who wants to maximize the use of this powerful app and you want to know everything about it, then the Premium Plan is just for you.

So what are the features for which you pay 99 RON/year (equivalent to $25/year)?

1. You can search in Office docs and attachments.

If you save your doc files (Microsoft Word) through Evernote (export them via email, clip them, or simply store them), you can search a specific word, phrase, or a whole document.

2. *Turn notes into presentations*

This feature is designed specifically for business people who are talking to small-medium audiences and want to show them their notes/ideas.

3. *Annotate attached PDF files*

This is also helpful and I wish this feature to be available for basic users, too. I think everyone has PDF files and using them within Evernote would have been useful.

4. *Scan business cards (Android)*

This feature is useful for Android devices just because the *Scannable* app isn't available for Android (I will discuss that app later).

So you can scan documents, receipts, business cards, etc., and attach them directly to your Evernote account. It's identical with the app used for iOS (*Scannable*).

5. *See related content to your notes*

If you work on a project that requires creativity and you run out of ideas, don't worry – Evernote will give you suggestions based on what you are working on – it will show you similar notes to yours.

6. *You get 10GB of monthly uploads (compared to 1GB with the Basic plan and 60MB with the Plus plan).*

In my opinion, this is too much for an individual account such as yours and mine. As 60MB was too low and filled really quick, 1GB is really more than enough – you can store audio files, PDFs, docs, emails, pictures, bookmarks, etc., and you won't reach the monthly limit.

Evernote has a special Premium Plan that is called Evernote Business – it allows a business to create a "Cloud" account that multiple individuals can use. The price per user is really high – it's 49 RON/month/user (~ $12.99/month/user) for up to 25 users.

Business people, entrepreneurs, and enthusiasts will prefer this Premium version of Evernote, whereas others will prefer the Plus plan.

A few months ago, Evernote only offered 2 plans – the Basic (Free) and the Premium. Since April 2015, they added a new one, the Plus Plan, and they have upgraded the Premium Plan, too (by adding a few new features). They have also limited the amount of monthly data. Before April, you had the possibility to upload unlimited data and after April, they added the 10GB/month limit (which is too much anyway).

Get free months of Premium Plan - Now Evernote has a special offer for people who promote this app (basically, affiliates).

If you bring 3 people who enter their emails there and download Evernote Basic (free) you get 10 points for each person, which is equivalent to 3 months of free Premium Plan (you can use that to test it out for free).

INVITE FRIENDS

Your first 3 referrals earn you 10 points each - enough for 3 months of Premium.

KEEP EARNING

Whenever a friend you referred buys Premium for the first time, you will earn 5 more points.

Then, for every person who registers and purchases Evernote Premium, you will earn 5 points which you can use to get extra free Premium months.

Tip – you need to provide their email to earn the points.

Chapter 5: The Basics – Notes, Notebooks, Stacks, and Reminders

Evernote is all about taking notes and organizing them into folders called Notebooks.

1. **Notes** – Depending on the plan you have, you can have notes from 25MB to 100MB.
   You can have an unlimited number of notes within your account and they sync on all your devices.

   Taking notes is an easy process. Go to the Evernote logo and click on "New Note" and this menu will appear (on all the platforms).

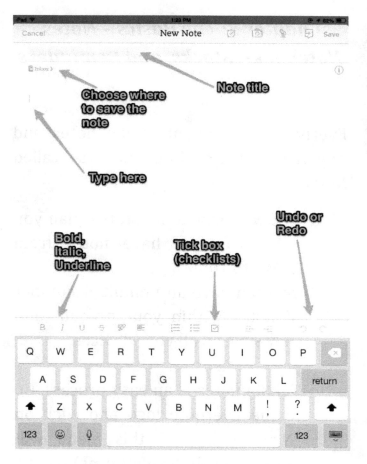

2. Notebooks – Every user has a preset "default notebook" and that's the place where your notes go if you don't choose your own directory.

You can store your notes into different notebooks and you can move your notes to other notebooks as well.

You have 3 types of notebooks:

a. Default notebook
b. Local notebooks
c. Synced notebooks

The *default notebook* is the place where your notes go if you don't choose a directory. My default notebook is called "Inbox" and to set it, you need to Right-Click on a Notebook -> Options -> Set as default Notebook.

Local notebooks are only bound to the device that you are creating them on – they don't sync across all the devices. It remains stored on only one device.

Synced notebooks can be store online through Evernote and can be used on all devices Evernote has been installed on.

3. Stacks – These are just like folders. You put the notes into a subfolder (a notebook) and you put the notebooks into a master folder (stack of notebooks). This will allow

you to organize your notes and
your stuff a lot easier.

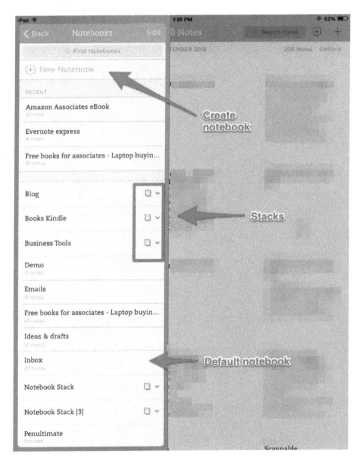

To create stacks, all you need to do is to
click on a notebook and drag-and-drop it

on another notebook and a stack will be automatically created. Then you can rename and arrange it how you want.

Chapter 6: Tagging Notes

From the very first moment you start using this powerful app, keep in mind that everything you create and store into notes can be simplified by adding multiple tags at once.

In the next chapters, I will cover how to clip websites, how to store notes from other applications, and so on, and the best way to keep everything in control is to add tags.

Let's say that you want to research about traveling to Europe. Every time you create new notes, add tags such as "Europe", "France", "Cheap", or "Must see".

This way, whenever you type "France", you will see notes related to France, cheap prices in France, places to visit in

France, things you could do in France, just by typing the keyword in the search bar.

Sometimes, tags can be more important than notes or notebooks. You could save or store data into notes and forget how you named that, in what stack are they and so on, but by tagging them, everything becomes easier.

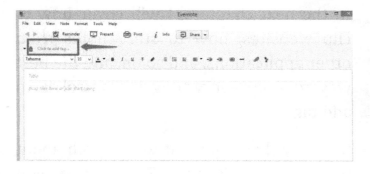

Chapter 7: Your Evernote Profile Page

Every Evernote comes with a profile page that can be accessed at any time from the Help bar as follows:

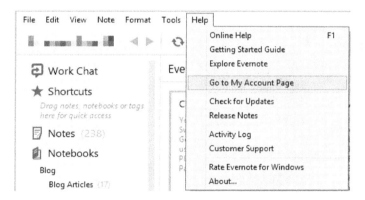

Here, you will find useful data and information such as:

- Amount of data used
- Your Evernote email address (custom email address created by Evernote)

- How long your account is available (if you purchased plans)
- Purchase history
- Gift Evernote Premium to a friend (if you have Evernote points)

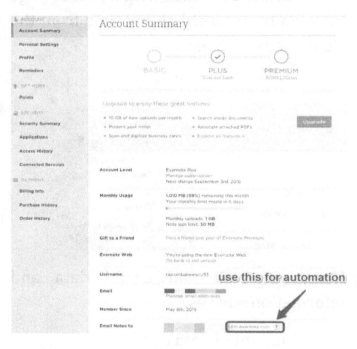

It's important to keep an eye on your traffic with Evernote, especially if you are using the Free Plan. When I was using

Evernote as a free user, I always thought, *How much data can I still use?* and later on, I found out where to look for that. It might sound easy, but when you don't have any experience with the application, it can be really tricky.

In the next chapter, I will explain how to automate email forwarding and you will need the Evernote email (see previous image).

To set up the email forwarding feature, go to your *Profile Page* (see previous chapter), copy the

Chapter 8: Automated Email Forwarding

I suppose everyone, at least once, has managed to get lost in hundreds of emails. Some of our emails are really important and we sort them, move them, or star them to know that it's something important.

An Amazon receipt, product warranties, special invitations, etc., are just few of the emails that require additional attention and should be saved or starred.

But what are you going to do when your "Starred" emails fill up and you don't know where you "put" an important email? You will have to scroll down to look for it and you will have difficulties in finding the right one.

And here comes Evernote – you can forward your important emails directly into Evernote as notes and those notes can be classified. Create a new stack of notebooks called "Emails", "Important Emails", "Forwarded emails", or whatever you like. Then, create notebooks with all your emails sorted – by month, by task, by priority, etc.

So, what are you going to do is to increase the sorting capabilities of your email. It goes like this:

Email -> "Marked as important" Email -> Starred Email -> Forwarded Email -> Sorted Email in Evernote

Obviously, don't forget to add multiple tags to each email to find it quicker when you need to.

I will show you how to do this for Gmail, as it's my primary email, but the same thing can be done for other platforms as well.

Step 1: Go to Gmail.com and make sure you are logged in.

Step 2: Go to settings icon and click again on settings.

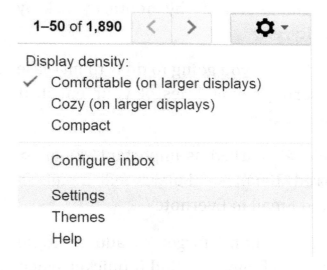

Step 3: You have multiple menus there. Go to the "Forwarding" section on the right.

Step 4: Go to your Evernote profile page and copy your unique Evernote auto-generated email. (See previous chapter)

Step 5: Put your email in the forwarding section and wait for the confirmation email.

Step 6: Go to Evernote in your default notebook and copy the link to your URL bar. Click confirm.

Step 7: Create a filter. Once you enable this, *all* your emails will be automatically forwarded to your Evernote email. To

avoid this from happening (it could get annoying), you can sort which emails to forward automatically.

Filter

From

To

Subject

Has the words

Doesn't have

☐ Has attachment

☐ Don't include chats

Size   greater than ⬍   MB   ⬍

I honestly use this if my emails contain attachments. Those emails come rarely and when they come, they may contain important data, photos, etc. In that case, I prefer to save them into my Evernote account.

Tip: Use multiple starring colors (you can have up to 6), I use green for emails not so important, but that I want to keep, yellow for those that I might need in the future, orange for those with greater priority, and red for those that are crucial.

You can sort your emails by using these options and you can manually forward the most important emails to your Evernote account. You can even create notebooks (into a stack) called "Green Starred", "Yellow Starred", "Orange Starred", and "Red Starred".

Organize them all once a week and you won't have a single problem with your emails. They all will be there when you need them (don't forget to add tags!).

Chapter 9: Web Clipper

From basics to premium, web clipping is a feature that is commonly used to store websites as articles, screenshots, notes, or bookmarks.

Web Clipper is a plugin for your web browser and it's indicated by the Evernote logo.

web clipper shortcut

In the right top corner of my browser (Google Chrome), I have my Web Clipper installed and ready to be used.

You can get the plugin from here - https://evernote.com/webclipper/?downloaded

Now, hot is it to use this feature – let me give you a couple of examples.

Whenever you click on the Evernote logo for Web Clipping, you will see this photo, which asks you:

- What do you want to clip?
- How you want to clip (article, screenshot, full page, or bookmark)?
- In what Notebook would like to save it?
- If you want to add tags on it
- If you want to add a remark

Now, I have created my own 'Inbox' Notebook for my Evernote and it's my default notebook. Whenever I want to save or note something down (randomly),

I choose this default inbox. Later on, when I start organizing my notes, I move them to other Notebooks or stacks of Notebooks.

I personally use the Full Page and the Screenshot features (especially the screenshot) and I save it for analyzing later. It really helps me to analyze certain things such as promoting a book in my business.

There's a KDP forum called Kboards in which authors post results, strategies, opinions, places to advertise, etc. So whenever I want to do a new promotion on a topic, I surf the whole forum and I find paragraphs or images that might help me.

I use Web Clipper to take screenshots of what I find interesting and store them as notes. I also add the tag 'promotion' or 'kboards' or something to quickly remember.

When I go to my Evernote dashboard and type 'kboards' in the search bar, the notes tagged with 'kboards' appear.

You can also save a full page and you can highlight what interests you most. That example is described in their official Web Clipper page, so I won't detail this too much.

For the Basic Free Plan, you will run out of storage quite quickly if you use this feature, but if you really want to save something important, you can use it.

This feature wasn't available for free users until April 2015 and I think they made it available for everyone to act as 'bait' for purchasing the Plus or Premium plans.

Web Clipper can also be used from your phone or tablet as well, having the same options as the web version.

Chapter 10: Importing Folders

Another useful de-cluttering tool from Evernote that can help you organize and store important information is the Import Folder tool.

You can basically import any kind of format, .doc, pdf, .xls, presentations, .txt, images, audio files, etc.

I have created a folder called "Imported Folders (Evernote)" to demonstrate and to illustrate the flow of the process.

First of all, this is the folder that I created – it contains a demo .doc (Word file), a demo .xls (Excel file), a demo image, and a demo .txt file (Notepad file).

The whole importing process is useful when you have dozens or hundreds, even thousands, of folders and documents and you want to store them to your Evernote app.

To save all those at once, here's what you need to do.

Step 1: Go to Tools -> Import Folders

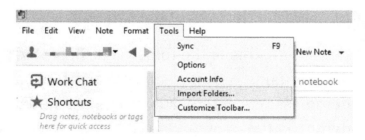

Step 2: Choose your Notebook where the imported folder should go. If you don't choose anything, it will go to your default

notebook. In my case, it will go to my "Inbox" notebook.

Step 3: Browse the folder you want to import (you can add or remove subfolders of the master folder).

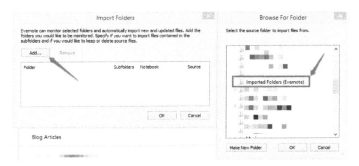

Step 4: Wait for a couple of minutes and then click on sync or wait for the app to automatically sync (usually after 5-10 minutes).

Step 5: Done. Here's your imported folder, all the 4 documents/files that I created are stored in 4 individual notes.

Inbox ▾

Demo 1.docx	Notepad for demo for Evernote. This should work	demo 3 - picture.png	Demo 4 - excell sheet.xlsx
W doc	3 minutes ago Notepad for demo for Evernote. This should work just fine.		**X** xls

Chapter 11: Scannable

Evernote itself is a paperless app that helps you note down your ideas on the go, wherever you are and whenever you want. But was that enough to stop them come up with new paperless idea? Well...no. Creativity is limitless.

The Evernote team developed a new application called Scannable, and as you have probably imagined, the application scans documents and photos using the camera. It's blazing fast, easy to use, and you can send the scanned documents directly to your Evernote application.

Who should use this app?

Everyone. Why should you carry all the receipts, tickets, lists and other papers with you when you can just take a snapshot and store them in your Evernote account?

Now, let me demonstrate the capability of this application. Here's a quick demo from my Scannable app from my iPad.

This is a photo (taken with a 5 Megapixel camera from my iPad Mini) of the original document.

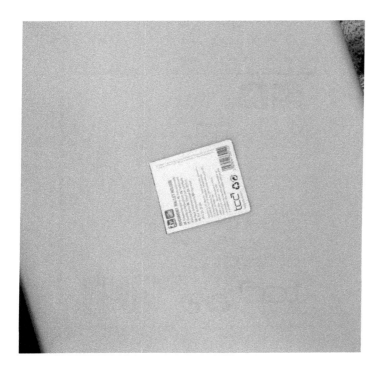

Now, with Scannable on the same device, the scanned document looks like this.

1 selected

2yr warranty

DOCUMENT WALLET HOLDER
DE Dokumententasche FR Porte-documents
IT Cartella portadocumenti ES Cartera para
documentación NL Document portefeuille
DK Rejse dokumentmappe CN 證件夾
PL Etui na dokumenty RU Портмоне

13 x 2 x 22 cm

Imported by TCC Global N.V., World Trade Center Amsterdam,
Zuidplein 84, 1077 XV Amsterdam, The Netherlands.
TCC Retail Marketing, Inc. 285 Riverside Avenue, Suite 325,
Westport, CT 06880, USA.
Made in China · Wyprodukowano w Chinach
Product Code: 1906109 · Job: 7263
Les conditions de la garantie sont consultables sur
le site suivant: http://www.tccglobal.com/fr/garantie/

The Elterhanser logo is a trademark of GROWN UP Licenses Ltd. and
may not be used without permission. ©2014 GROWN UP Licenses Ltd.

tcc
tccglobal.com

5 023041 330122

🔗 Scannable Document

📩 Mail   💬 Message

📗 Evernote   📤 Export

🖼 Camera Roll   ••• More...

Meeting   Recent   Share

I think it's absolutely amazing how this application scans documents without a single flaw. I don't have the greatest camera, so imagine how it looked if I had a 13 Megapixel shooter. It automatically adds a black and white contrast to view it better.

The only issue with this app is that it's available only for iOS devices, so if you have an android device, you will need to purchase the premium plan to scan (see previous chapter regarding Premium Plan).

Soon after you take a photo of the document, you can easily send it to Evernote and store it as a note. If you have multiple documents, store them into a notebook and maintain the organization.

Chapter 12: IFTTT Recipes and Evernote

IFTTT, or If This Then That, is a website that collects dozens of popular applications and creates "recipes" for using and interconnecting them.

Those dozens of applications can be connected between them, and Evernote is obviously among them. By connecting Evernote with apps from IFTTT, you will be able to automate a lot of processes that would take too much time to do them by yourself.

Each individual application has several actions and each individual action can connect to other several actions from Evernote, allowing you to choose from over 10,000 recipes (just for Evernote).

How to create a recipe

Step 1: Go to http://ifttt.com and sign up using your email.

Step 2: Click on "Create a recipe" and you will a big list with icons and applications (including Evernote).

Create a Recipe

ifthisthenthat

Step 3: Choose a trigger. Let IFTTT know what you want it to do for you – choose the action.

Choose Trigger Channel

Search Channels

Step 4: Click on Evernote and connect with it. Evernote will request authorization from one day up to one year. I use this app regularly, so I chose the final period to be one year.

🐘 Choose a Trigger

New shared note link
This Trigger fires every time you share
a new public note link.

Step 5: Choose what action you want IFTTT to do for you – create a new note in the specified notebook, create an audio note or just save the URL of what you want into a new note.

Example – I chose *Weather* (IF weather) – the trigger *"tomorrow's temperature drops below 0 degrees Celsius"*. Then, I chose the action within Evernote to send me a note in my *"Weather News"* notebook.

If you find some recipes very interesting or more important than you think you can create the same note If Weather Then Email, so you will receive an email if the weather changes. Regarding the Weather feature, you can choose triggers such as "If the temperature rises", "If humidity changes", "If wind blows with X speed", "If UV rays are violent", "If tomorrow rains", "If tomorrow snows", etc.

I find the automations for weather, email, notes, important files, receipts really, really handy to use. It saves me a lot of time and thus, increases productivity.

Here's a list of what IFTTT can do for you automatically:

- Send receipts from Amazon to your Evernote notebook (you can create a new, dedicated notebook).
- Connect Evernote with your Google Calendar to get notes for upcoming events.
- Automatically copy important files from Dropbox to Evernote whenever you add something new to your Dropbox folder (if your monthly plan allows you).
- Get notifications or create a note if the weather changes (temperature drops below X degrees, get notified if it will rain or snow, etc.). I use this

recipe if the temperature drops below 0 degrees Celsius.

- Create a new note with every new starred email.
- Send a message from your phone number to another phone number when you require (when you to a specific task).
- Create a new note with every new photo or video from your phone.
- Monitors your AC from your home – It will send you a message if the temperature exceeds your preset values.
- Monitors the thermostat from your home and sends you a message when temperature drops or increases abnormally.
- Save Instagram or Facebook photos on your request.
- Tell you when you run out of battery.

- Save a song's name from SoundClound when you like a new one.
- Connect with Siri from your iOS device and sync.

And the list goes on and on. You have more than 10,000 recipes to choose from just for Evernote plus thousands of other recipes for interconnecting the other applications.

Chapter 13: Swipes

As Evernote has become popular and useful to more than 100 million people, third party apps started to create integrations and shortcuts with Evernote.

GAIN THE FULL OVERVIEW OF
YOUR TASKS

One practical app is Swipes, which basically allows you to create *To Do Lists* and manage them – yellow bullet for 'needs to be done', red for 'delayed', and green for 'done'.

Now, by using Evernote all the time, you can create lists (as notes) in the app and what Swipes allows you to do is to import those notes and manage them.

Step 1 - First of all, you need to download the Swipes application from http://swipesapp.com/

Sign up and choose your platform (Mac, iOS, Android, or Windows). What I will present to you next will be on iOS.

This app works best on mobile devices – Android or iOS devices.

Step 2 – Sync with Evernote from your device (in my case, my iPad). Go to the 'Integrations' menu and choose Evernote. This will show up and you need to grant authorization.

Step 3 – Import notes that contain lists. What the application will do now is to convert your list from the note to a *To Do List.*

I have imported a note from my Evernote account and it has been automatically converted into a *To Do List.*

You can start adding new tasks by tapping on the *Add button* below, you can mark them as *Done* by swiping the screen to the right, or you can mark them as *Delayed* by swiping your finger on the left.

Just in case you mark a task *Delayed,* you have multiple options to re-schedule it for later.

The app is really useful, especially if you have long lists and lots of tasks to do.

Chapter 14: Penultimate

This app is automatically integrated with Evernote. Once you sign up and download it, everything you do will be saved as notes directly into your Evernote default notebook.

Penultimate is a handwriting application that is quite easy to use. In fact, it's the best handwriting digital application I have ever used. It's responsive, even with your fingers and you have multiple options while you type (zoom, colors, pen type, etc.).

It's good for students or for people who prefer to take notes without writing on paper. If someone dictates to you, you can type very fast and natural.

You have unlimited space to write on, it automatically adds pages, so you don't need to worry if you "run" out of ink or paper.

Here's a short demo on my iPad.

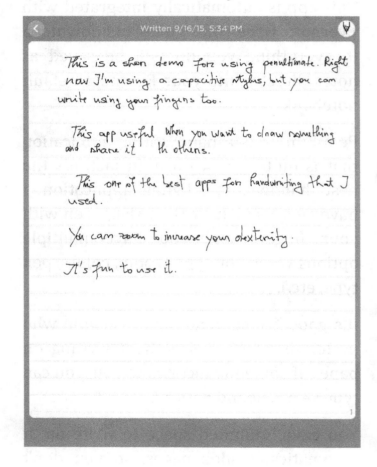

Chapter 15: Skitch

This application (designed by Evernote) is a photo editing application, but what you can do with it is quite useful.

It helps me because I can take a screenshot and then modify it – crop, insert texts, colors, add arrows (best feature), and highlight parts on it.

Obviously, it's integrated with Evernote, so everything you modify or create with this app will go directly into your default notebook. All you need to do is to download the app and you're ready to go.

In the menu of Skitch, you have multiple options to choose from:

Crop – You can always resize a photo and save it later.

Screenshot

Arrows – You can use arrows of different sizes and colors, you can drag them on the screen where you want to. You can undo every action and you can edit if you are not satisfied with their final position.

Texts - You can add text boxes.

Circles, Ellipses – Just like in the photo below, you can add any kind of forms or colors when you need to highlight something.

Rectangles – Similar to the circles and ellipses, you can use the rectangle tool to highlight texts or images. I use this when I want to explain something or when I want to save something into my Evernote account.

Environmentally friendly - Wikipedia, the free encyclopedia
https://en.wikipedia.org/wiki/**Environmentally_friendly** ▾
Environmentally friendly, environment-friendly, eco-friendly, nature-friendly, and green are marketing terms referring to goods and services, laws, guidelines and policies that inflict reduced, minimal, or no harm upon ecosystems or the environment.
Regional variants - Europe - See also - References

Pixelate – You can blur any parts of a document or photo before you share it with others. It's useful when you make a tutorial using photos and you want to censor personal information.

Original photo

Environmentally friendly - Wikipedia, the free encyclopedia
https://en.wikipedia.org/wiki/**Environmentally_friendly** ▾
Environmentally friendly, environment-friendly, eco-friendly, nature-friendly, and green are marketing terms referring to goods and services, laws, guidelines and policies that inflict reduced, minimal, or no harm upon ecosystems or the environment.
Regional variants - Europe - See also - References

Images for environmentally friendly   Report images

More images for environmentally friendly

Pixelated photo

Highlight – Mark parts of texts that you liked or that you need with a color and store them in Evernote.

Add icons and emoticons (mobile version)

Change colors

Ideas for using this application

- *Create tutorials using images and adding arrows and indicators to them.*
- *Highlight websites for later use in your projects.*

- *Crop images before storing them in Evernote – fast and easy.*
- *Share your images with others on social media – it's a fast way to edit photos in a basic manner.*

Note – I actually used Skitch to create this book, it really helps and it's easy to use.

Chapter 16: 20 Ideas and Suggestions for Using Evernote

#1 - Quick access to lectures for students

I don't know much about you, but when I was a student, I didn't know about this app. Real notebooks, tons of papers, projects (on paper) were mandatory at my university.

It wasn't the best in the country but it was a decent one. However, we had to take notes on real papers and I have lost at least half of them by lending them to different colleagues or friends. A waste of time, energy and trees to make that paper.

With Evernote, all of that would have been easier. Even if I had to write down the lectures, I could have stored them using the Scannable app and nothing would have been lost. (See previous chapters about Scannable).

#2 - Keep a notebook with annual taxes and bills

Another handy way to use this app is to create a list with all your annual taxes (property tax, car tax, insurance, etc.) and set reminders for each of them one week before you need to pay them. Important documents should have a special place to store them, and the best place is Evernote. This way, you have them with you all the time.

#3 - Create your own cookbook

Whenever you see or try a delicious recipe, you might want to save it somewhere. I'm sure you went to a friend at least once and he gave you something delicious that he made and you asked him about the recipe. If he just tells you, you probably forget about it until you get home or you mess up the ingredients.

Evernote will be there when you visit the next person and you can type down the recipe and store it to your dedicated cookbook notebook (or stack of notebooks).

You can create a stack of notebooks called "Cookbook" and then insert notebooks on different topics - desserts, side dishes, sauces, etc. In each notebook, you can add your notes with the recipes and also add tags (examples: name of the person who gave you the recipe, tag if you tried that or not, tag when you want to try it, etc.).

#4 - Create your "to do" travel list

Start your vacation with an in-depth plan. Create a new stack of notebooks called "Travel" and add a notebook in it with your destination. Add notes with the hotels' details, your bookings, the restaurants you want to try out, and the places you want to see. Create notes for each day. You can use Web Clipper to capture a few descriptions, photos, and recommendations from Trip Advisor.

Also, make sure to scan your plane tickets, just in case you lose them. When you check in, all you need is a proof and the codes required for the flight.

#5 - Record yourself (audio) and save as notes

Every time you have an idea, you hear a song, or you want to share some of your moments, creating an audio note is the best thing you can do. You can have a look at them later when you get home. You are probably going to an event and you want to record the speech. Do so and store it in your notes.

#6 - Create a maintenance notebook for your car

When was the last time you changed the oil? You have no idea what the exact date is, right? Whenever you change a part, the oil, the timing belt, gaskets, or whatever technical feature that you adjust, note that down and always set a reminder when to go to a service.

This way, you don't have to always look in the car's maintenance book (service repair notebook). Keep everything easy and paperless.

#7 - Create a shopping list

More than once, I have gone shopping for something and when I get there, I completely forget what I needed to purchase. This happens when you need to buy dozens of products and you have a 99% chance of forgetting at least one or two of them.

Create a shopping list like this one, this way, you won't waste time thinking of what you bought and what you haven't. Save time and energy.

You can share this list with your family through Evernote. If you go shopping and your mom remembers that she forgot to tell you to buy something, she can send you an updated list.

#8 - Create your own wish list

I am sure you want to buy things that you love, things that you can't afford to buy all at once, but creating what and when to buy will keep you motivated and in full control. I have my own wish list that I keep as a notebook in Evernote and those things are basically expensive electronics such as headphones, a MacBook, the latest iPhone, a piece of software, etc. That wish list can be totally different, but the idea is to create one and to keep it up-to-date.

#9 - Create a personal diary

Writing down your thoughts, whether they're positive or negative, will help you discharge your emotions and at the same time, you will create some memories.

Writing a diary or a journal as a hobby has been done for decades, even centuries, but this app now allows you to do this whenever you want, wherever you are. You don't need the diary with you or a pencil to write with, you just need...your phone, tablet, or laptop. For those who were already practicing this, Evernote has just simplified their task.

#10 - Store your medical data

Health is the most important thing in our lives and it needs to be kept in control all the time. Whenever you go to a doctor, take a pill, take a supplement, or have tests done (such as blood analysis), create a note and save into a notebook called "My Medical History" or "My Health".

#11 - Declutter your email inbox

I am the kind of guy who spends 70% of the day in front of a computer - learning, studying, working, writing, advertising, etc. I have subscribed to over 100 websites (including Amazon), which send me tons of emails on a daily basis. To make everything easier, I try to "mark as important" my emails or to "star" them. But even using those functions, I end up filling my email box with things I don't need anymore.

A standard email allows you to classify your emails into "Inbox", "Sent", "Important", and "Spam". You don't have any other ways to sort out your emails. With Evernote, you can set up the forwarding tool to automatically send important emails to Evernote and save them as notes.

Those notes can be saved into your diversified notebooks or stacks (medical situations, car insurance, receipts from

PayPal, flight tickets, business emails, collaborations, etc.).

#12 - Set goals (weekly, monthly, and yearly)

In Evernote, you can create your own monthly goals and all you need to do is to stick to them. Simply create a stack of notebooks called "Goals", then create a notebook with each year or each month. In that notebook, create notes with each month or each week (it's totally up to you how you want to diversify it).

#13 - Convert Evernote into your digital notebook for handwriting

As a student, you have to carry physical notebooks, papers, manuals, books, etc., all the time. You can simply scan the pages you need before your lecture (to eliminate the books), you can install Penultimate to have something to write on (a cheap capacitive stylus would be recommended to write faster, almost naturally).

You can store unlimited eBooks on your device without having too much weight in your backpack. To do all this, you should have a tablet that has an 8" screen or higher (10" would be best).

#14 - Work on specific projects

Whatever project you need to start, Evernote is the best place to start drafting. If you're a business person, or a public speaker, Evernote can help you present your notes (Premium Plan required for this). When I start writing a new book, a new blog post, or I have new ideas, Evernote is the place I start.

#15 - Create a journal of your experiences

Whenever you eat something great, do something great, help someone and you want to keep that memory, note that down in Evernote. Create a notebook and include pictures, audio notes, and text notes. This way, you can create lots of memories.

#16 - Become an online bargain hunter

There's no doubt that a lot of people make money from buying and selling things such as real estate properties. Hunt those properties down and store the best ones that you find in Evernote. This will help you decide which one to buy later.

#17 - Track your monthly expenses

Without a doubt, life is expensive and no matter how much money we have, if we don't control how much money we spend, we will end up having massive credit card debt. To avoid that, create a list with your daily/weekly/monthly/annual budget. Track everything you spend depending on the budget you have.

#18 - Organize your online research

Now, if you have been using Evernote for a long period, try to organize your notes once a week. Delete useless and old notes that you don't want to keep anymore.

#19 - Store important photos as notes

Capture every important photo as a note instead of writing it down as a text note. You will save valuable time. If you have just the Basic Free Plan, you should save it as a text note to preserve your monthly storage, but if you have the Plus or the Premium Plan, take a photo and store it in your notes.

#20 - Create your own widgets with IFTTT

A simple and productive way to enhance productivity is to create your own widgets (for weather, email, smartphone, etc.). You are the one who will customize that (see how in the previous chapter).

Evernote will do what you tell it to do – store notes, store URLs, etc., and all of that automatically.

#21 – Import your old folders to Evernote

If you have documents and other old stuff that you don't use a lot but you want to save it somewhere, Evernote is the place to save them.

#22 - Go completely paperless

We should always think of Mother Nature and we should try to protect the Earth however we can. Let's go paperless, because we now live in an era when technology allows us to go completely paperless - Evernote, eBooks, notes, etc.

Paper = cut trees. Cut trees = less oxygen. Less oxygen = pollution and toxicity in the atmosphere.

Let's use Evernote as our primary "Notebook" in which we write, organize, and use all our ideas.

Other books by Ryan Stevens

Amazon Associates

Kindle Publishing PRO

Entrepreneur Enhanced

More to come soon

I invite you to check out my blog. I will upload content about Internet marketing, self-publishing, productivity, applications, and email marketing, and I will be more than glad to share some of my experiences with you for free.

The blog is under construction until 1st November 2015.

www.entrepreneurenhanced.com

Write a review

I know that most of you will skip this part, but I would really appreciate if you would take the time to write a short review for this book.

It really helps me learn from the any mistakes that I made in this book, and it will help me gain more visibility and more exposure on Amazon.

No matter what thoughts you may have, please take just one minute to write them down.

Last word

Thank you for purchasing this book and for taking the time with to read it entirely.

I hope that now you are able to use Evernote and you will start taking advantage of it every day.

As technology evolves and Evernote will change, I will come back with updates for you every 6 months.

In this book, I will also include an invitation to subscribe to my blog once it's ready and you can follow me and learn new things for free.

Talk to you soon,

Ryan